Knight Book of Things to Make and Do

Knight Book of Things to Make and Do

Leslie Marshall

KNIGHT BOOKS
Hodder and Stoughton

ISBN 0 340 16176 0
Copyright © 1973 Leslie Marshall
This edition first published in 1973 by Knight, the paperback division
of Brockhampton Press Ltd (now Hodder and Stoughton Children's Books),
Salisbury Road, Leicester
Third impression 1975

Printed and bound in Great Britain
by Richard Clay (The Chaucer Press) Ltd
Bungay, Suffolk

CONTENTS

INTRODUCTION

The things in this book can all be made by children. The materials are reasonably cheap to buy or can be found in most homes. Coloured paper, thin card and glue suitable for sticking these can be bought from any shop which sells art materials. Egg boxes, toothpaste tube boxes and cardboard cartons can be saved instead of thrown away.

All of the things can be made without too much mess on a kitchen table covered with plastic cloth or layers of newspaper.

Simple instructions are given for each model. The easier things are at the beginning of the book and those which are more difficult, or which will take longer, are at the end.

Follow the instructions carefully and read them right through before you start work. Choose your colours carefully. You can try two or three things in different colours, and add your own ideas when you have had some practice.

Always work slowly and very carefully. You want the result to be neat and tidy. Make sure that your hands are clean, that your scissors are sharp and that you are using the right sort of glue, and the right sort of paint. There is a list of materials at the front of the book to help you.

I should like to acknowledge the help given by Elizabeth Hufton in building the shape of the book, Timothy for his inspiration for many of the models and David and Sarah for their help in the photography.

6

MATERIALS

White cartridge paper
Coloured paper
Thin coloured card (manilla)

Egg boxes
Cardboard toothpaste cartons
Cereal boxes
Cardboard tubes
Felt scraps
Sharp scissors (these are safest if they are not pointed)

Emulsion paint
Poster paint or powder colour
Rapid drying silver enamel
Felt tip or fibre-tip pens
Wax crayons or coloured pencils

Sticky tape
Glue for sticking paper and card

Paste is not usually strong enough for models. If you buy
glue for sticking cardboard it will stick paper also.
P.V.A. glue is best and is not messy. It can be used with
water to thin it down.

Thin canes can be bought from florists

Tissue paper, silver paper, buttons, shells, beads, wool,
string, raffia and many other bits and pieces can be
added to your models with strong glue to make them
interesting.

NEWSPAPER TREE

Materials

Sheet of newspaper   Scissors
Piece of card   Paint
Brown paper   Sticky tape or glue

Take a folded sheet of newspaper and roll into a tube.

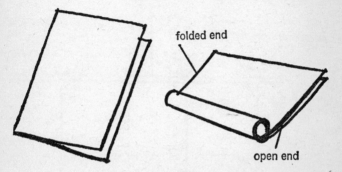

Cut a fringe around the open-ended top about 13 cm deep.

Push up at the folded end with your first finger. The paper will now spiral out at the top.

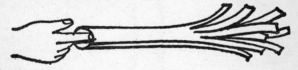

Snip three equally spaced cuts about 4 cm apart at the bottom of the trunk and fold the flaps out. Glue to card to make the tree stand up.
Stick brown paper round the trunk.
You could make a tree with coloured paper or spray it with paint.

FISH MOBILE

Materials

60 cm long stick about ½ cm thick (balsa wood will do)
Thin white card
String, cotton or thread
Scissors
Paint

Draw your fishes on to the card. Two could be exactly the
same size as the diagram, 10 cm × 5 cm; the other two twice
as big.

The drawing is purposely within squares so as to make it easy to enlarge. So for your big fishes draw a rectangle 20 cm × 10 cm and divide into eight squares, then draw the design.

On the other hand you may wish to draw your own designs, in which case look at some pictures of fish to discover more fish shapes and patterns.

Cut out, make a hole for cotton, then paint or decorate with silver paper.
When hanging your fish from the stick you may have to adjust them slightly so that they all balance.
When finished the mobile should be tied to the banister on the landing to hang into the hall below.

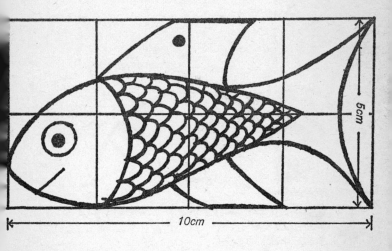

TWIZZLER

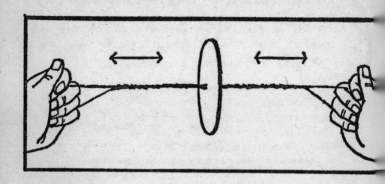

Materials

Stiff card
Strong thread
Pencil

Scissors
Paint
Paint or felt tips

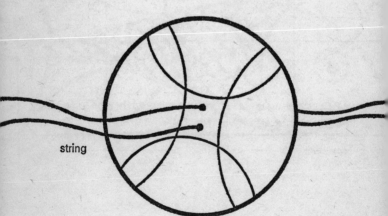

string

Draw the circle with a radius 5 cm. You may have to stick two pieces of card together to get your twizzler stiff enough.

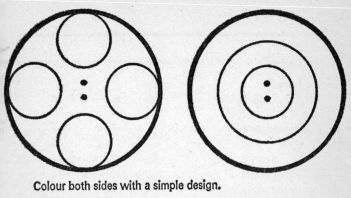

Colour both sides with a simple design.

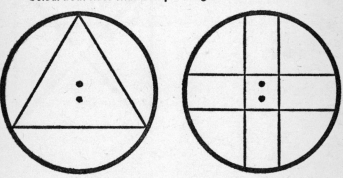

Make two holes one cm apart and put thread through as shown. To make the twizzler work swing the circle over and over to wind it up, then slacken and tighten in order to keep it spinning.

WINDMILL

Materials

Stiff paper
Ruler and pencil
A cork or small piece of balsa wood

A pin
Thin stick
Scissors

Draw diagonals in pencil and cut down 7½ cm.

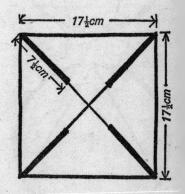

Fold corners a, b, c, d to the centre.

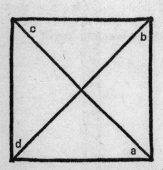

Put a pin through the centre corners.

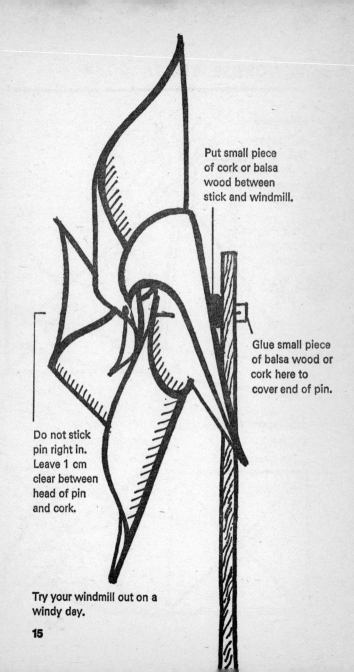

Put small piece of cork or balsa wood between stick and windmill.

Glue small piece of balsa wood or cork here to cover end of pin.

Do not stick pin right in. Leave 1 cm clear between head of pin and cork.

Try your windmill out on a windy day.

15

NEWSPAPER HATS

Materials

Newspaper
Coloured paper
Tissue paper
Pencil, ruler
Scissors

Glue or staples
Felt pens
Paints
Other things to decorate

Fold the paper.

Fold down the corners.

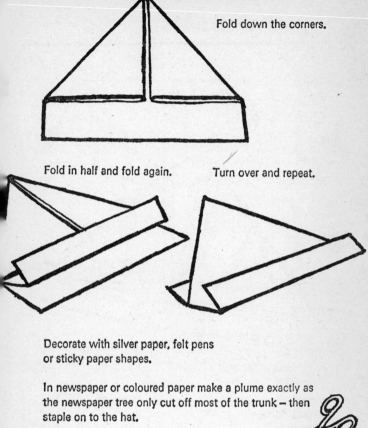

Fold in half and fold again.

Turn over and repeat.

Decorate with silver paper, felt pens
or sticky paper shapes.

In newspaper or coloured paper make a plume exactly as
the newspaper tree only cut off most of the trunk — then
staple on to the hat.

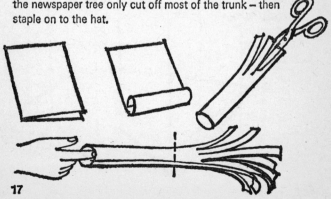

RING OF DANCING DOLLS

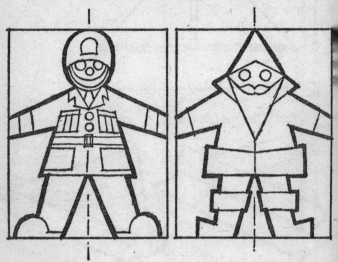

Materials

Piece of stiff paper 32 cm × 10 cm
Scissors, pencil, ruler
Crayons or felt tips

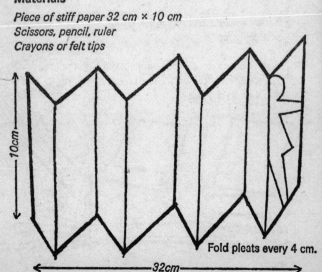

10cm

Fold pleats every 4 cm.

32cm

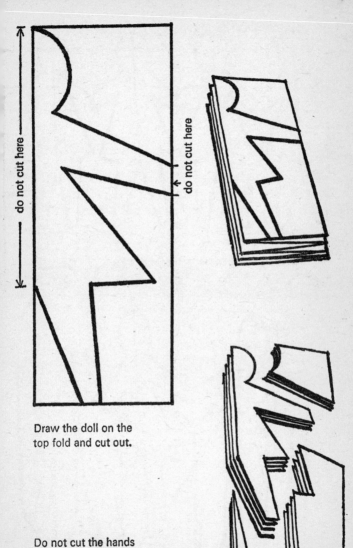

do not cut here

do not cut here

Draw the doll on the
top fold and cut out.

Do not cut the hands
or your dolls will
fall to pieces.

Pull out and stick hands together in a circle.

You can make dolls of any sort of person you like.
Try a clown, a policeman, or a Father Christmas.

CROWN

Materials

Thin card
Tracing paper
Coloured paper

Pencil, scissors
Glue, paint

Trace the diagram opposite and cut it out. Place on a piece of folded paper, draw round it and cut it out double thickness.

You now have a pattern to draw round.

Unfold.

Cut out a piece of card 62 cm × 10 cm. Divide into sections. Use your paper pattern to draw the shape out four times.

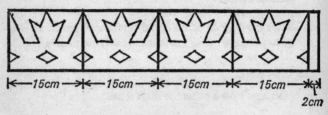

|←— 15cm —→|←— 15cm —→|←— 15cm —→|←— 15cm —→| 2cm

Fold the card to cut out the diamond shapes.
Glue a strip of coloured paper on the inside, behind the holes.
Paint, or decorate with silver paper.
Staple or glue the ends together to make the crown.

SIT UP BEAR

Materials

Brown card or stiff paper 20 cm × 11 cm
Felt pens, glue
Scissors, tracing paper

Trace the diagram over the page and cut out.

The body of the bear.

Trace and cut out.

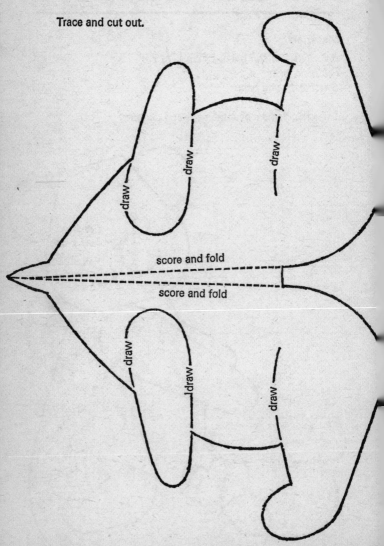

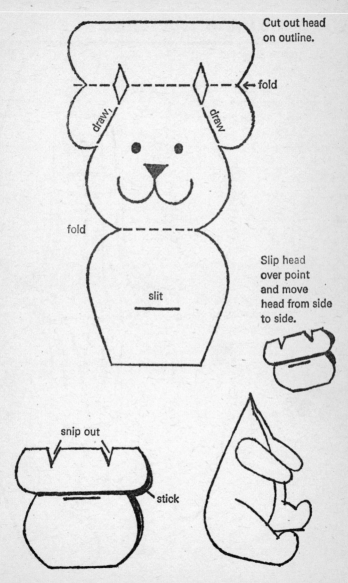

Cut out head on outline.

← fold

draw, draw

fold

slit

Slip head over point and move head from side to side.

snip out

stick

27

CHRISTMAS LANTERNS

Materials

2 pieces of brightly coloured paper 20 cm × 26 cm
Glue, scissors, ruler, pencil
Odds and ends to decorate

Take one piece of paper.
Measure and draw 10 strips
2 cm wide and cut up
to $4\frac{1}{2}$ cm from top.

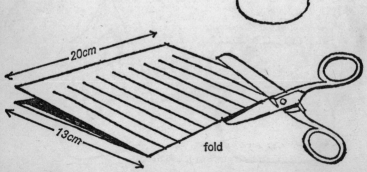

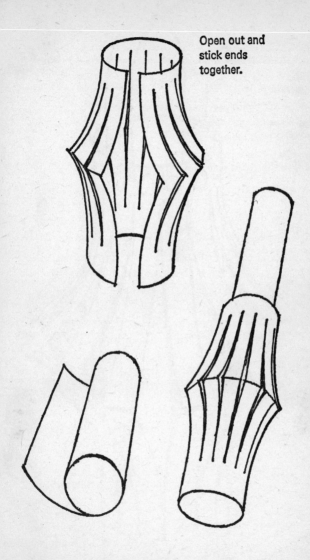

Open out and
stick ends
together.

Roll up the other sheet of paper
and push through the centre of the lantern.

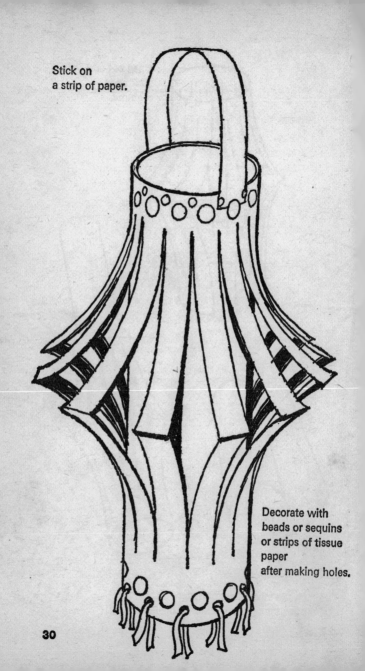

Stick on
a strip of paper.

Decorate with
beads or sequins
or strips of tissue
paper
after making holes.

MASK

Materials

Paper or thin card
Pencil, scissors, tracing paper
Elastic or tape, felt pens, crayons

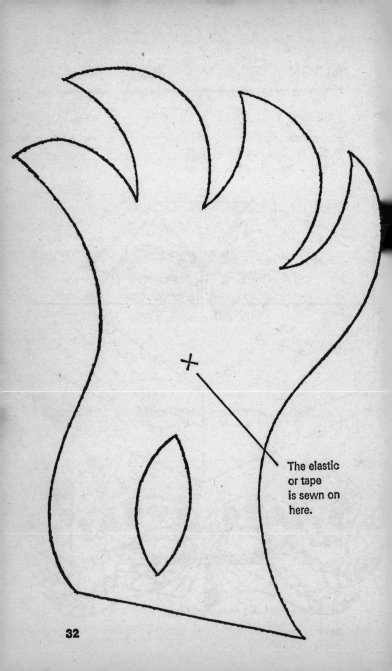

The elastic
or tape
is sewn on
here.

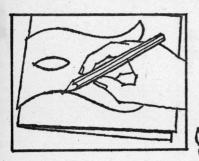

Trace the diagram opposite and cut it out, place on a piece of folded paper or card, draw round it and cut out double thickness.

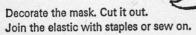

Decorate the mask. Cut it out. Join the elastic with staples or sew on.

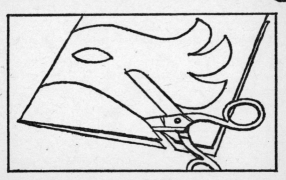

Now try and make a different design.

COLOURED PAPER STARS

Materials

*Several squares of stiff paper in assorted colours at
least 15 cm*
Pencil, scissors, felt pen

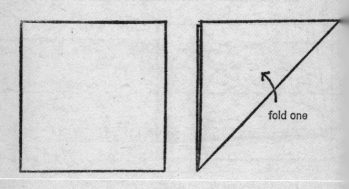

fold one

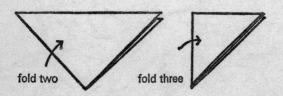

fold two   fold three

Fold the square three times.

Using the corner of a book as a guide draw a right angle as the dotted line.

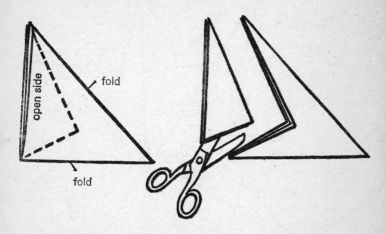

Cut carefully, then open the star out.

Press the folds of the star so that one fold goes up and the next goes in, all the way round.

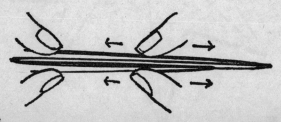

Now try some big ones up to 35 cm.

You can hang them on thread in various sizes or stick
a small one on a card by the tips to make a Christmas card.

PAPER FLOWERS

Materials

Pencil, scissors, drawing pins
Squares of coloured paper of different sizes
Milk bottle tops, thin canes

Start with a square 15 cm and fold like this.

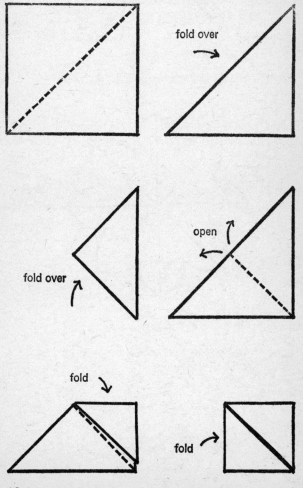

fold over

fold over

open

fold

fold

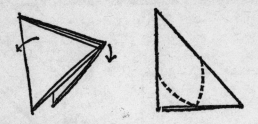

Draw a petal tip similar to the dotted line and cut out.

Open it out.

Repeat with a smaller square 7 cm for the rosette, in a different colour.

Take a metal foil milk bottle cap and mould into a smooth dish shape with your thumbs.

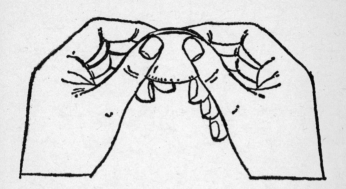

Push in a drawing pin and stick on to the rosette through the centre.

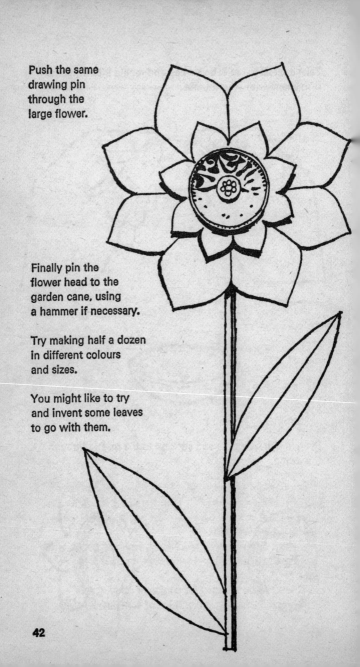

Push the same
drawing pin
through the
large flower.

Finally pin the
flower head to the
garden cane, using
a hammer if necessary.

Try making half a dozen
in different colours
and sizes.

You might like to try
and invent some leaves
to go with them.

NAPKIN RING

Materials

Cardboard tube
Elastic band
Pencil, sharp knife
Raffia, felt
Coloured paper or paint

Measure 4 cm along the tube. Put an elastic band round this point. Cut the tube carefully with a sharp knife on a hard board. Paint or cover carefully with paper, or bind with raffia, glueing the ends.

Make a flower as explained in the previous pages, either in coloured paper or in felt, and sew or staple it to the ring.

These can be very gay for parties or other special occasions. Perhaps you can think of some more ideas.

CUT OUT PAPER BIRDS

Materials

Coloured papers   Sharp knife
Ruler   Crayon or felt tips
Scissors   Pencil

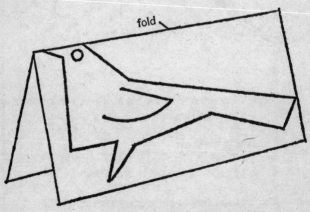

fold

Draw the bird on one side of the paper.

Try your bird like this first.

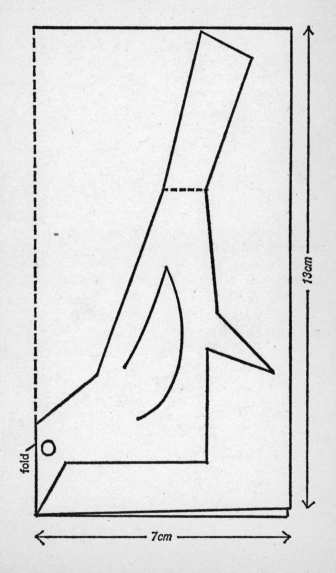

13cm

fold

7cm

It is better to ask an adult to cut the wing shape with a sharp knife.

Curl the wing out from the body. Curl the tail out, and stand on feet and tail, then decorate.

Try making birds of different shapes. You could make them in different coloured paper, or decorate with felt tip pens. Here are some ideas.

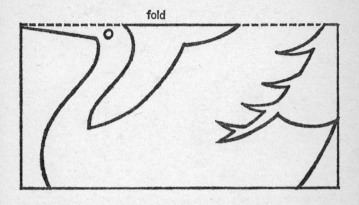

fold

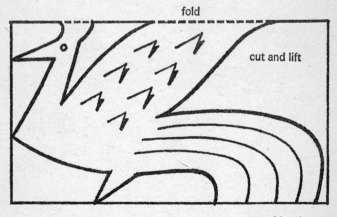

fold

cut and lift

cut with scissors

A POP UP SCENE

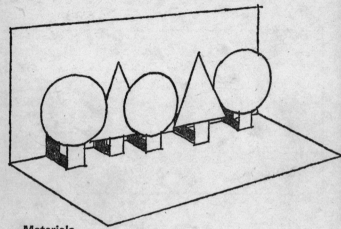

Materials

Stiff paper or thin card 30 cm × 20 cm
Coloured papers or pencils, scissors, ruler

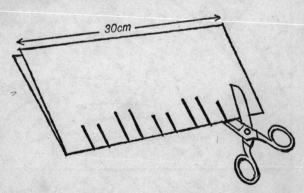

Fold the sheet of paper lengthways and snip short strips as shown. Make 5 trunks about 2 cm wide, 3, 15 cm up and 2, 3 cm up. Open and push up.

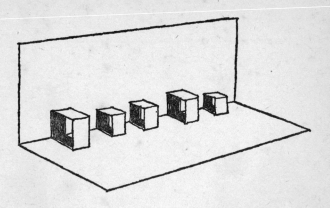

For the trees
Cut out three circular shapes about 5 cm in diameter

and two triangles.

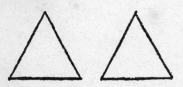

Colour, and stick to the trunks to make trees.

ELEPHANT

Materials

Stiff white paper
Tracing paper
Coloured paper

Scissors, pencil
Felt tip pens
Ballpoint pen

Trace the diagrams, turn the tracing over and go over the outline with a soft pencil. Put the tracing on your paper and go over the outline with a ballpoint pen. The tracing will come off on to the paper.

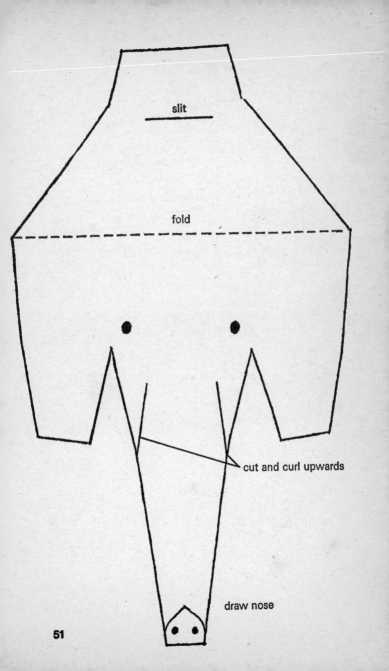

slit

fold

cut and curl upwards

draw nose

51

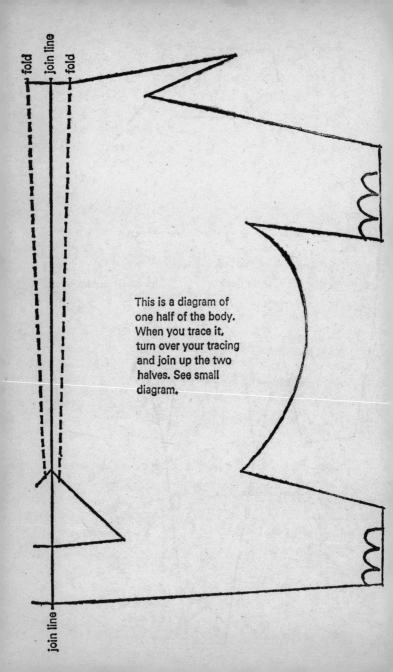

fold

join line

fold

This is a diagram of
one half of the body.
When you trace it,
turn over your tracing
and join up the two
halves. See small
diagram.

join line

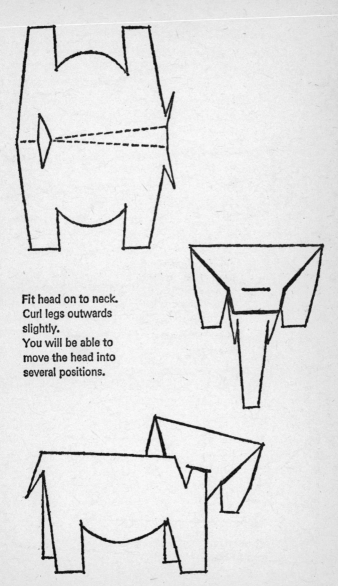

Fit head on to neck.
Curl legs outwards
slightly.
You will be able to
move the head into
several positions.

DACHSHUND

Materials

Cardboard tube from centre of toilet roll
Brown wrapping paper
Strong glue
Nail scissors

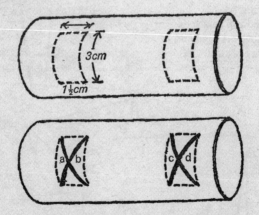

First mark out two rectangular shapes in pencil on the roll 3 cm × 1½ cm.

Then make crosses from each corner.

Now slit these and cut with the nail scissors, then bend
out the flaps a, b, c and d — we now have four tiny feet.

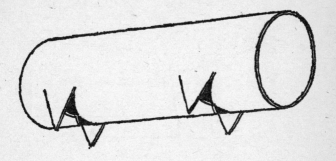

Take a piece of brown wrapping paper 10 cm × 11 cm and
wrap around the tube sticking along the bottom edges only.

Cut out a tail and glue inside the end of the tube. You
will have to curl the end upwards slightly.

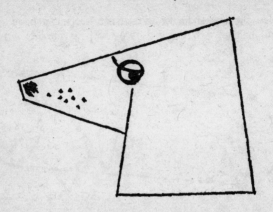

Trace or copy this diagram on to a piece of folded brown wrapping paper — head and nose along the fold.

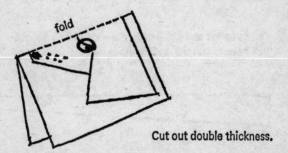

fold

Cut out double thickness.

Cut out and put glue behind each ear.

Position the head carefully as the drawing and stick on to the body.

GREEK HELMET

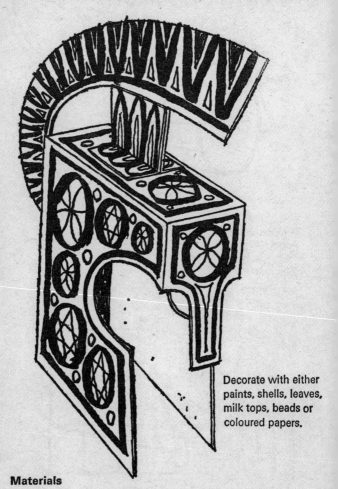

Decorate with either paints, shells, leaves, milk tops, beads or coloured papers.

Materials

Large (16 oz size) cereal box which will fit over your head
Scissors, ruler, pencil, glue, silver enamel paint, poster colour

There are three pieces to the helmet. First make the helmet, then the stand which holds the crest, and then the crest. The three pieces are then glued together.

To help you draw the design.
Draw lines on your box as shown by dividing into halves, then quarters and then sixteenths.

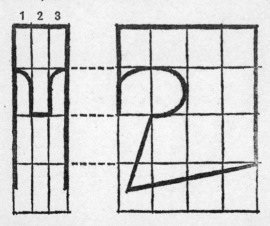

The end of the box is divided into three equal parts across the top and four parts down. Cut out and paint in silver enamel. Two coats will completely cover up the printing.

Fold up.

The Stand which
holds the Crest.

slit

Cut this shape out of
a piece of cardboard.
Fold on the dotted lines
like the picture on the
opposite page. Paint silver.

Fold up.

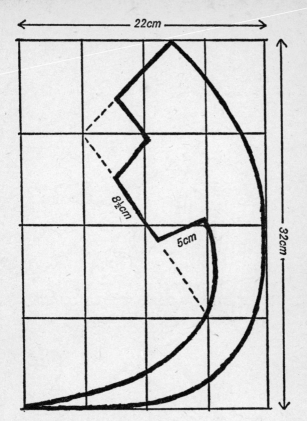

Cut the crest out of card (another large box will do) and paint in a bright colour.

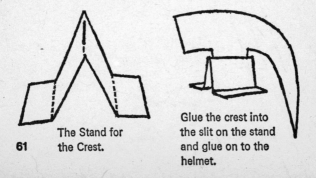

The Stand for the Crest.

Glue the crest into the slit on the stand and glue on to the helmet.

HOBBY HORSE

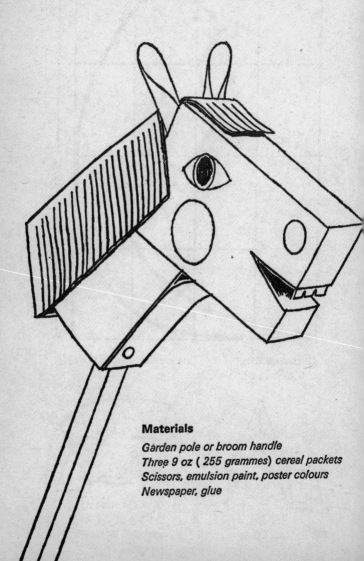

Materials

Garden pole or broom handle
Three 9 oz (255 grammes) cereal packets
Scissors, emulsion paint, poster colours
Newspaper, glue

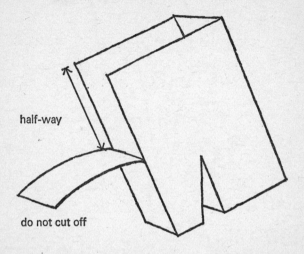

half-way

do not cut off

Cut half way down the end of one box as shown, then cut out the mouth and join to a second box.

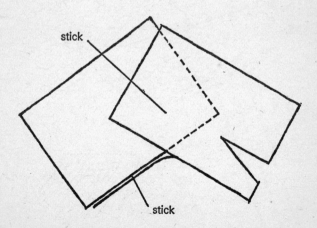

stick

stick

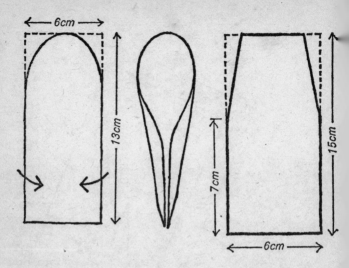

The ears are cut out of card.
Put glue on the bottom of each ear and stick between the boxes.

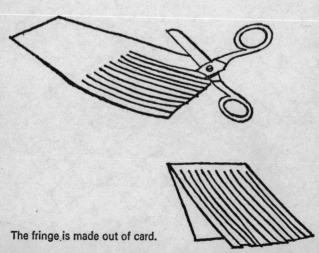

The fringe is made out of card.

Glue the fringe and the ears in place.

For the mane you need the third box. Cut as shown.

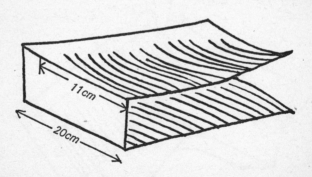

Fold a scrap of card as shown and glue to the neck.
Stick on the mane as shown.

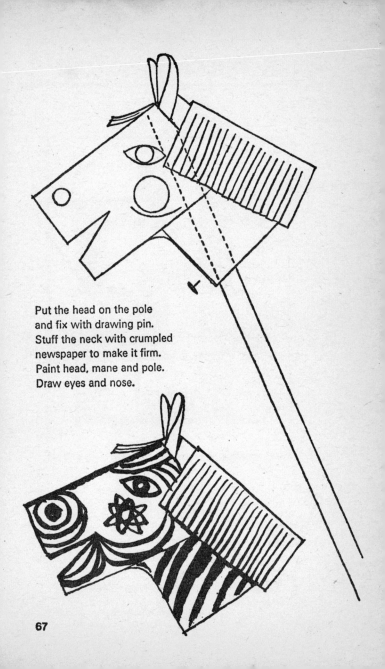

Put the head on the pole
and fix with drawing pin.
Stuff the neck with crumpled
newspaper to make it firm.
Paint head, mane and pole.
Draw eyes and nose.

PAPER AND CARD PATTERN

Materials

White cartridge paper
One piece of thick coloured card 13 cm × 16 cm

This is a simple repeating pattern needing careful
measuring and folding.

Draw one of these carefully on stiff paper and fold as shown.

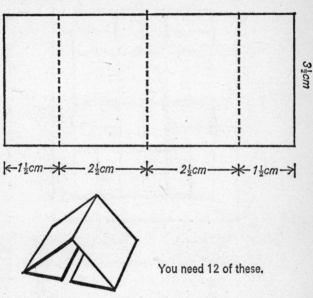

|←1½cm→|←———2½cm———→|←———2½cm———→|←1½cm→|

$3\frac{1}{2}$cm

You need 12 of these.

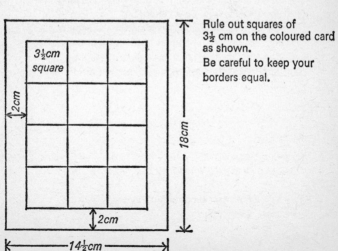

Rule out squares of $3\frac{1}{2}$ cm on the coloured card as shown.
Be careful to keep your borders equal.

$3\frac{1}{2}$cm square

2cm

2cm

18cm

|←————14½cm————→|

Stick the triangle shapes on the squares as shown.

With the light shining on them these look very interesting. Try making them in coloured card, or in paper-backed foil (you can get this from an art shop).

If you want to hang the pattern on the wall you can stick four matchboxes on the corners at the back of the picture and then stick those on to a large piece of brightly coloured card. Glue a piece of cord on the back to hang your pattern up.

GLOVE PUPPET

Materials

A matchbox
White or pink paper
Glue
Wool

Scissors
A paper bag
Felt-tip pens or crayons

Cut a hole here big enough for your first finger.

Stick pink paper round the matchbox leaving the bottom open.

Cut a triangle of card for the nose, fold it and stick it on.

The paper bag should just be large enough for your hand to fit inside. The head fits on to your first finger. Cut the sides of the bag and glue together.

Finish the face.
Add wool for hair.

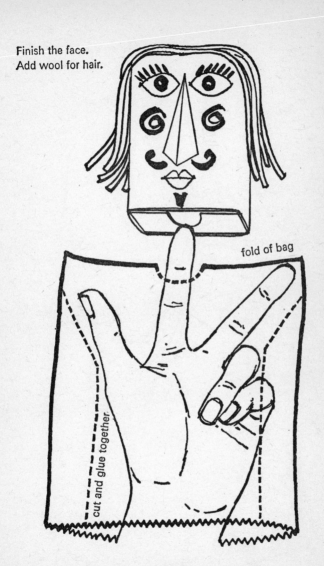

fold of bag

cut and glue together

HAND PUPPETS – PRINCE AND PRINCESS

Materials

Toilet roll tubes, coloured papers, white paper
Cake doilies, ruler, scissors, glue

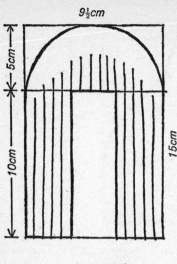

Cut out the hair from a piece of coloured paper 9½ cm × 15 cm.

9½cm

5cm

10cm

15cm

Cut strips.

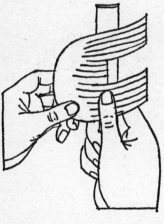

Curl the hair between the finger and ruler, pulling the ruler down the paper.

Stick on the tube.

Cut out eyes in black paper,

lips in pink paper.

Arrange and stick on to the tube.

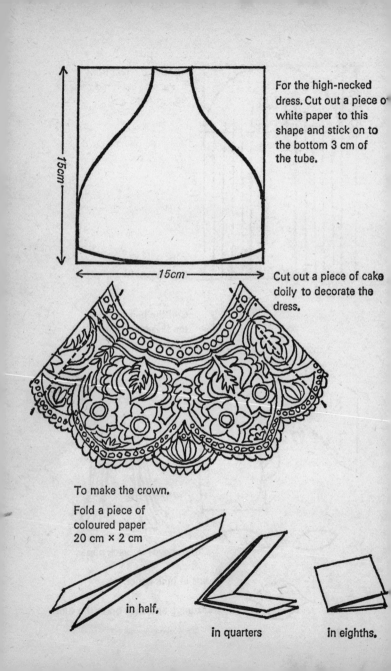

For the high-necked dress. Cut out a piece of white paper to this shape and stick on to the bottom 3 cm of the tube.

15cm

15cm

Cut out a piece of cake doily to decorate the dress.

To make the crown.

Fold a piece of coloured paper 20 cm × 2 cm

in half,

in quarters

in eighths.

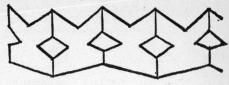

Snip with scissors and open out.

Now try and make a prince.

PENGUIN

Materials

One toilet roll tube
White paper 14 cm × 13 cm
Orange paper 5 cm × 5 cm
Black paper 11 cm × 11 cm
Glue
Pencil

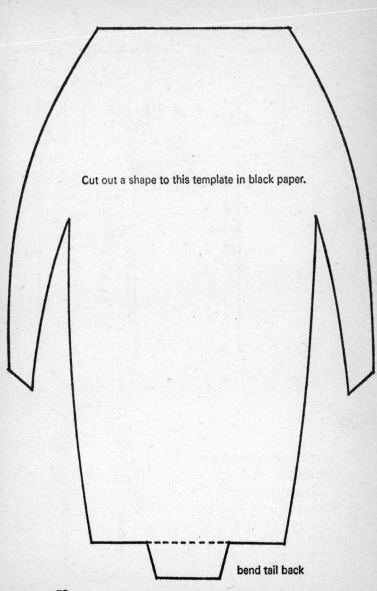

Cut out a shape to this template in black paper.

bend tail back

79

Take a piece of white paper
14 cm × 13 cm.
Wrap it round the tube and glue it.

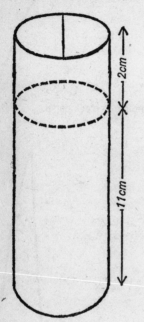

2 cm

11 cm

You should
have 2 cm at
the top.

Squeeze this in
as shown.

Wrap the black body round the tube
and glue.

Trace head and cut out in black paper.
Draw the eye on white paper with black pen, cut out
and stick on. Cut out the beak in orange card.
Stick head on to tube.

Trace and cut out feet in orange card. Tuck between the
white paper front and cardboard tube.

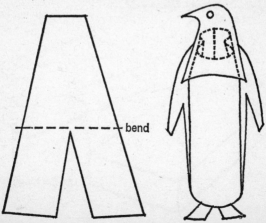

bend

CASTLE

Materials

Four toilet roll tubes
Two flat boxes about 16 cm × 11 cm
Cartridge paper
Scissors, glue
Ruler, paint

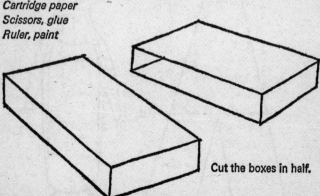

Cut the boxes in half.

One box is to be the entrance.
Draw the doors.

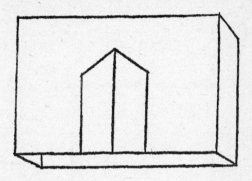

Cut doors and bend inwards.

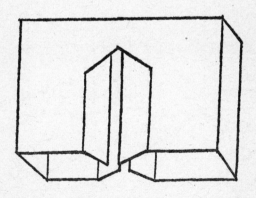

Repeat on other side.

Put the toilet rolls at the corners and the boxes in between.
Stick with strong glue.

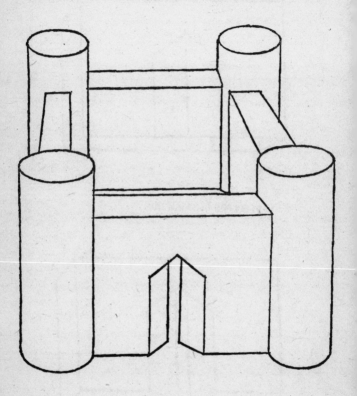

For the wall battlements cut 4 strips of cartridge paper
13 cm × 3 cm and score two lines 1 cm apart from the top.

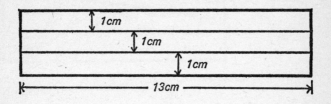

Now bend.

Mark off *1cm* ticks ½ mm down.

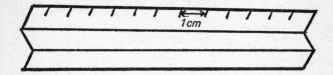

Snip down the
marked edge
with tip of the
scissors.

Cut out alternating pieces.

Stick battlements to walls.

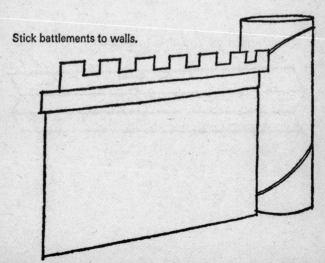

For the towers cut four strips of cartridge paper
15 cm × 3 cm.
Draw ticks along the top, 1 cm apart.

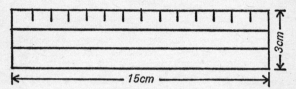

Snip with scissors as before and cut out as for
battlements.
Overlap the two ends and stick together.

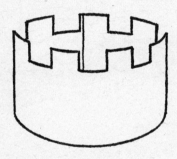

Stick the battlements on to the towers.
Paint stonework on the castle in grey-green.
Window slits can be painted on or cut out.

Perhaps you could invent a drawbridge?

MODEL THEATRE

Materials

Two cereal boxes, they must be the same size
Old magazines, comics, toothpaste carton
Glue, scissors, pencil, paint or coloured papers

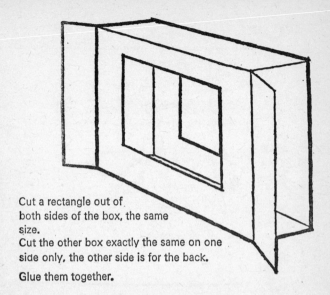

Cut a rectangle out of
both sides of the box, the same
size.
Cut the other box exactly the same on one
side only, the other side is for the back.

Glue them together.

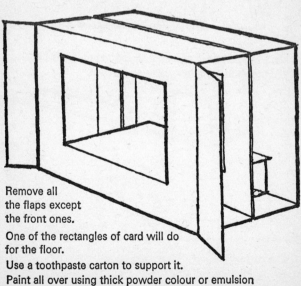

Remove all
the flaps except
the front ones.

One of the rectangles of card will do
for the floor.

Use a toothpaste carton to support it.

Paint all over using thick powder colour or emulsion
to hide the printing.

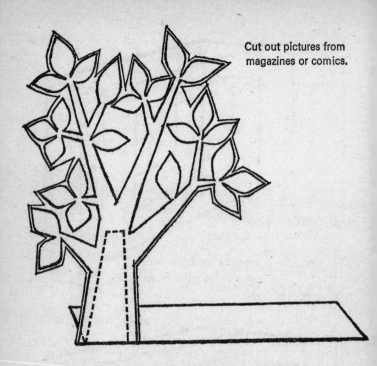

Cut out pictures from magazines or comics.

Make long tabs out of thin card, carton board will do.
Paint them in the same colour as the floor.

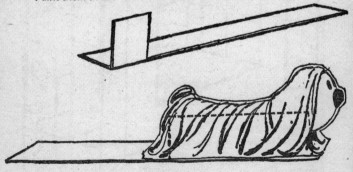

The part which you stick to the picture
should be as big as possible.

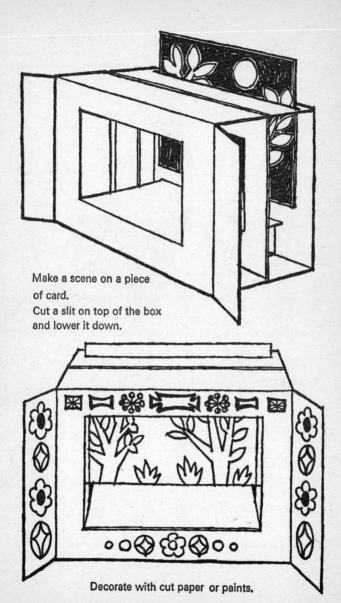

Make a scene on a piece
of card.
Cut a slit on top of the box
and lower it down.

Decorate with cut paper or paints.

CAMEL

Materials

Cardboard tube out of toilet roll
An egg box
Paper, string, wool, glue, scissors
Tracing paper, felt-tip pens
White cartridge paper, paint

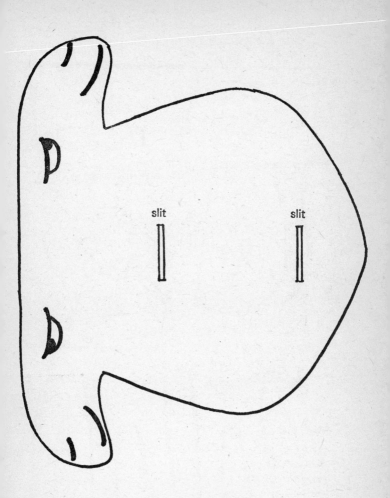

slit

slit

Trace the head on to a piece of white paper.
Draw the face. Cut slits.

Put a spot of glue here and press the nose together and then the neck.

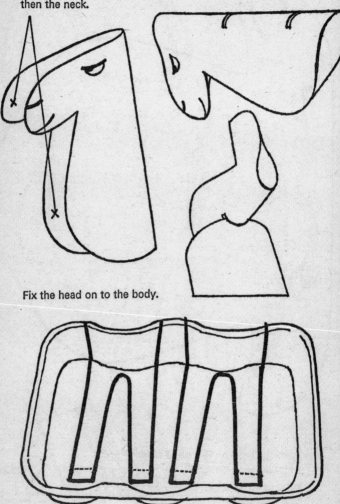

Fix the head on to the body.

The legs are made from the lid of the egg box. Cut them out.

Glue the camel's humps
on to the body. Make a
string tail and paint.

Wrap wool round
a piece of card.
Snip off at the bottom.
Tuck fringe of wool under humps.

95

CRAB

Materials

A pressed card egg carton
Toothpaste carton
Paper, scissors, pencil
Glue, knife, paint

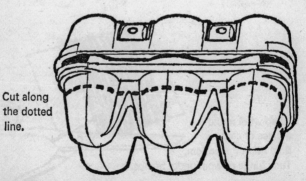

Cut along
the dotted
line.

The claws are made from the toothpaste carton.
Take off the flaps.

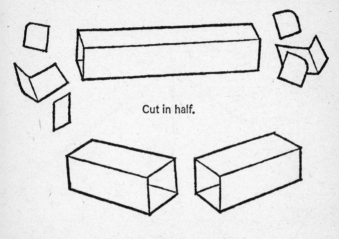

Cut in half.

Draw a triangle on both sides

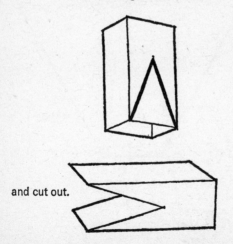

and cut out.

You need two of these claws.

To attach the claws to the body you need a piece of paper the same size and shape as the one below. Trace it and cut it out in stout paper.

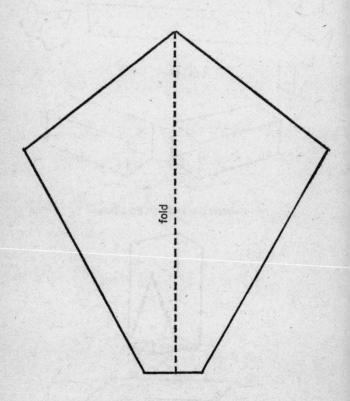

fold

Push the cone of paper into the claw and glue.

Glue to the inside of the body.

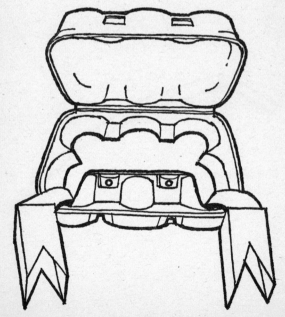

To make eight legs cut eight strips of paper 12 cm × 4 cm.
Roll tightly and stick the edge.

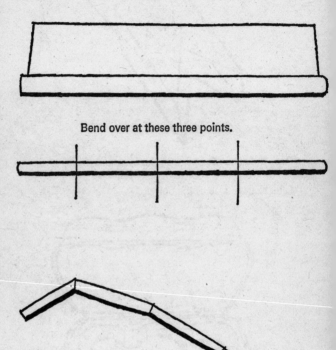

Bend over at these three points.

Glue four legs to each side of the body.

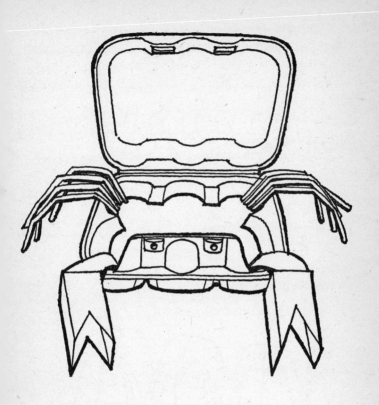

Paint the eyes white with black pupils.
Glue the lid of the box down.
Paint the crab in red or pink,
and decorate.

CROCODILE

Materials

2 pressed card egg boxes
Toothpaste carton
Thin card (old cereal boxes will do)
Stiff paper, paint
Scissors, glue, cellulose filler

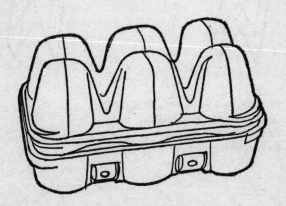

Choose two boxes with the same sort of shape.

Cut 10 sections off the egg boxes with a knife or sharp scissors. If you put an elastic band round and draw a line round with a pencil you can see where to cut.

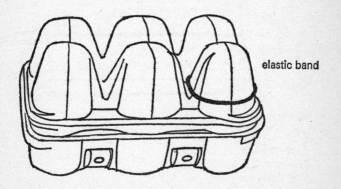

elastic band

Stick them together in twos. Don't worry about cracks, these can be filled later.

In the middle of the egg boxes you will find two little sections. Cut these off and join.

Stick them all together,

with the two small sections on the end.

To make the jaws
Remove one of the ends from the toothpaste carton.

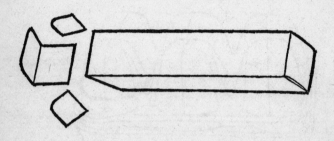

Draw a triangle on the widest sides of the carton.

Cut out with scissors.

Make the nostrils from a scrap of card.

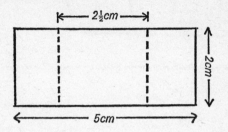

Use a small coin to draw the round ends.

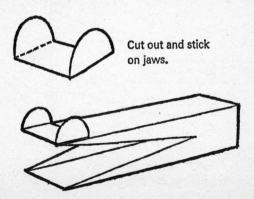

Cut out and stick on jaws.

Cut off the flap from the egg box

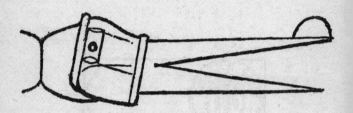

and stick it on to make head and eyes.

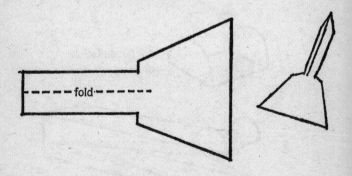

fold

Trace this drawing of the feet and cut out of card.

Glue legs between the cracks on the body.

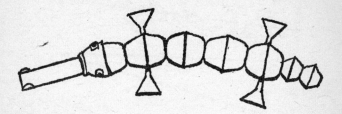

The tail is made from card 19 cm × 8 cm.

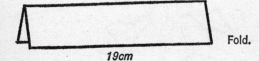

Fold.

19cm

Draw a line

and cut to a point.

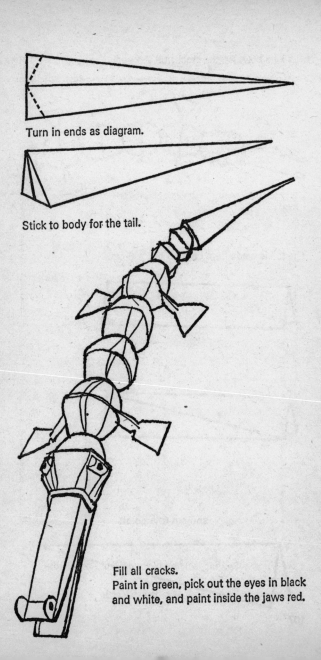

Turn in ends as diagram.

Stick to body for the tail.

Fill all cracks.
Paint in green, pick out the eyes in black
and white, and paint inside the jaws red.

JUMPING JACK

Materials

String, scissors, pencil, ruler
Paper fasteners, card, paint

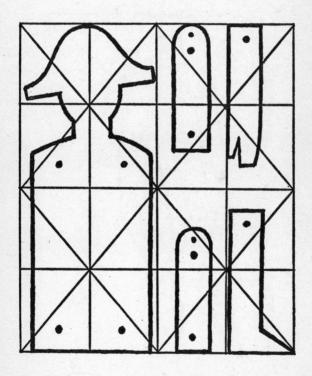

Follow the diagram. Make holes with knitting needle.

You can make the puppet twice this size.

This is how the back of the dancing doll looks.

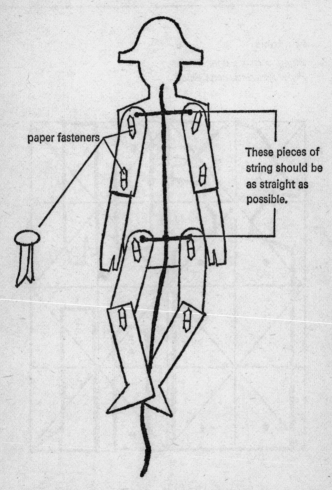

paper fasteners

These pieces of string should be as straight as possible.

Pull the string, and the legs and arms will shoot out. Release, and they will return. If they don't, check the holes for roundness.

HOUSE AND FURNITURE

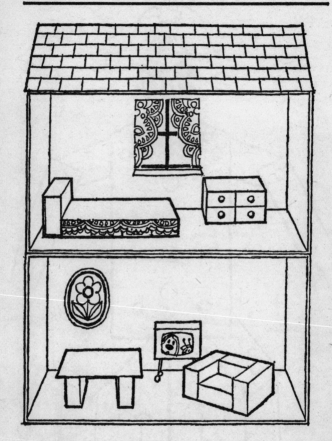

Materials

A number of matchboxes
Two cardboard boxes the same size, shoe boxes are ideal
Gift wrapping paper with a small pattern
Plain coloured paper, oddments of wallpaper, cake doily,
magazines, stiff card, pins, pencil, ruler, scissors, glue

Glue the two boxes together on their sides.

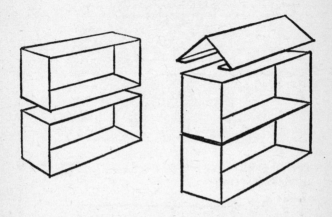

Cut a piece of card for the roof.

gable end

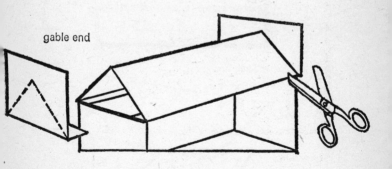

You could now cover the walls and roof with paper or paint bricks on the wall and tiles on the roof.

You can make all the furniture with matchboxes.

Cover the matchboxes with patterned paper before you stick them together.

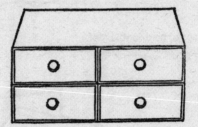

Push in pins or paper fasteners.

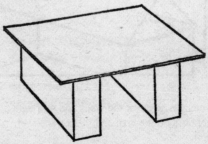

You could paint the table and cupboard.

Toothpaste cap and ballpoint pen cap
together make a table lamp.

Old comics, matchbox and push pins
together make a television set.

Make a family of dolls to live in the house
out of pipe cleaners and odds and ends.

A SAILING SHIP

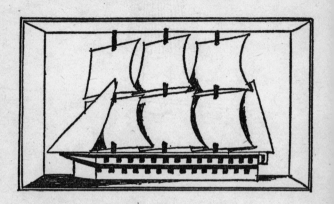

Materials

A standard size toothpaste carton   Pencil, ruler, scissors
Plastic drinking straws   Knife, black fibre-tip pen
Stiff white paper   Blue coloured papers, shoe bo.

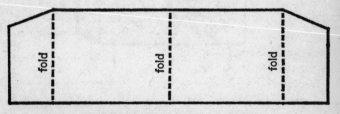

Cut a piece of paper like this to fit the end of the
carton for the bow of the ship.

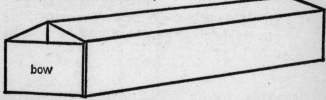

bow

Trace and cut out in stiff paper.

Fold and push into carton above bow.

Cut out in stiff paper exactly
as template.
Fold and stick on the other
end of the carton for the
stern of the ship.

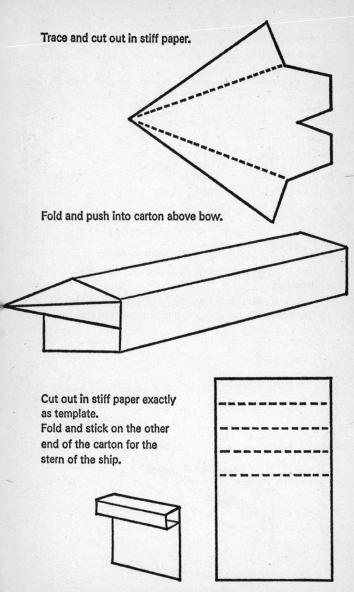

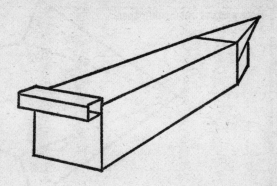

Cut out a piece of stiff paper 7½ cm × 14 cm.
Draw in the gun ports in black as shown with a fibre-
tipped pen.
Score (that means make a scratch mark with the point of
the scissors) down the line of fold, using a ruler as a
guide.
Fold.

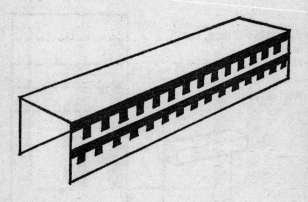

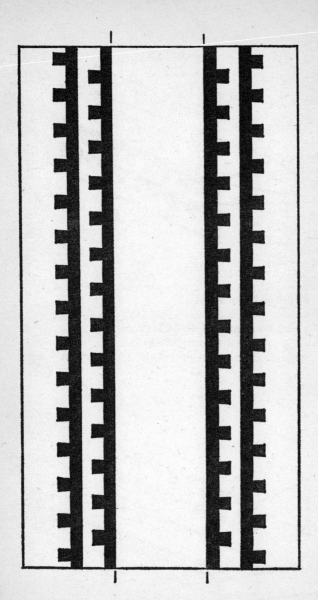

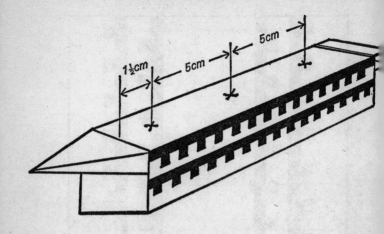

Stick on to the hull.

Mark the points on the deck in pencil.
Make an X with the point of a knife.
Press in three plastic drinking straws for the masts.

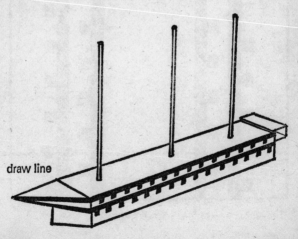

draw line

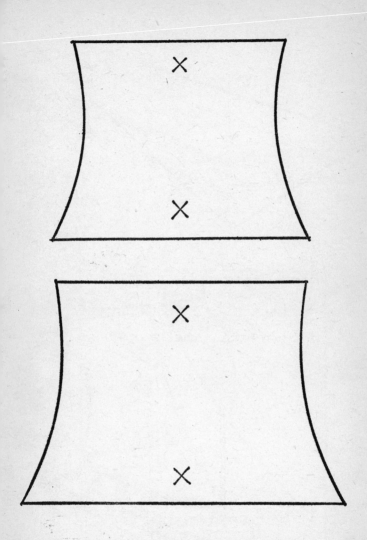

Trace and cut out three sails of each size shown.
Mark the X with the point of a knife.

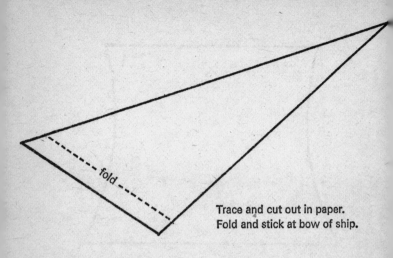

Trace and cut out in paper.
Fold and stick at bow of ship.

Copy as diagram and stick on stern.

To make the sea for your ship to sail on turn a shoe box on its side and put the ship inside. Use coloured paper for the sea and sky.

PLANE

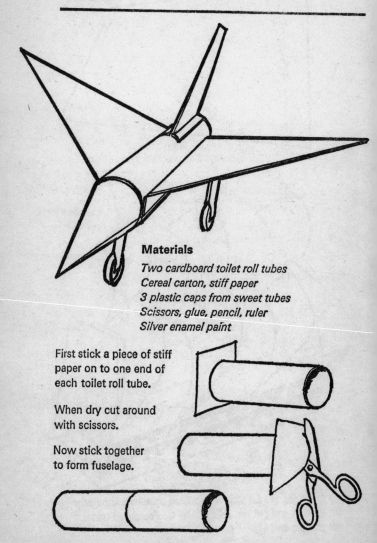

Materials

Two cardboard toilet roll tubes
Cereal carton, stiff paper
3 plastic caps from sweet tubes
Scissors, glue, pencil, ruler
Silver enamel paint

First stick a piece of stiff paper on to one end of each toilet roll tube.

When dry cut around with scissors.

Now stick together to form fuselage.

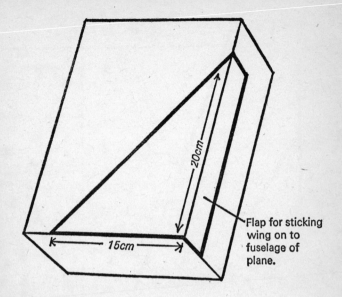

20cm

15cm

Flap for sticking
wing on to
fuselage of
plane.

Cut the other wing from the other side of the carton and
glue on to body.

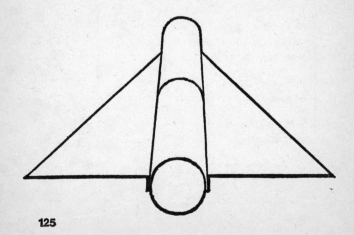

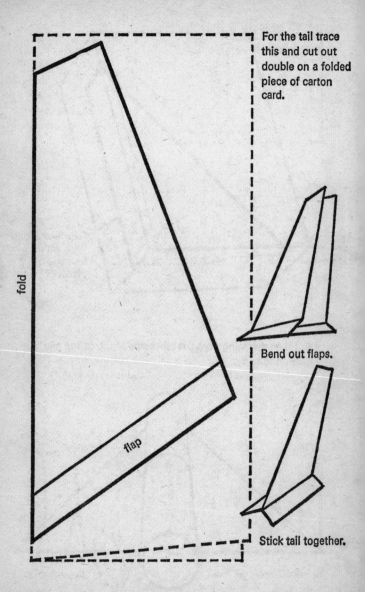

For the tail trace this and cut out double on a folded piece of carton card.

fold

flap

Bend out flaps.

Stick tail together.

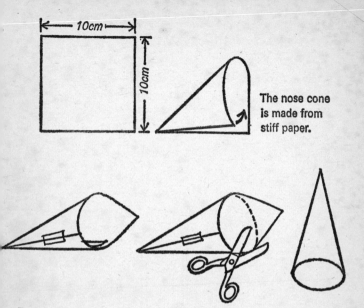

The nose cone
is made from
stiff paper.

The wheels are all made in the same way.
For the nose wheel you need a piece of carton card
3 cm × 4 cm, and for the other two wheels the card is
3 cm × 6 cm.

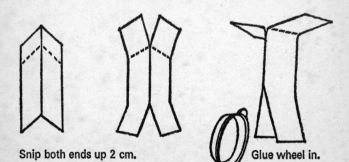

Snip both ends up 2 cm.   Glue wheel in.

Stick the tail to fuselage.
Glue edge of nose cone and push in.

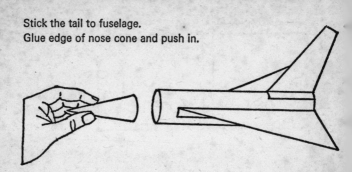

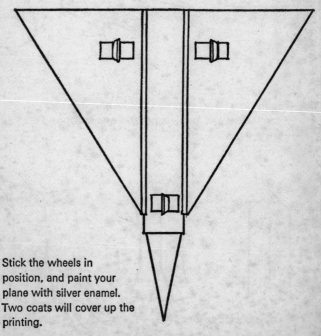

Stick the wheels in
position, and paint your
plane with silver enamel.
Two coats will cover up the
printing.

128